aReN't tHEY
LoVeLY WHeN
tHEY'Re
asLEEp!

'Ann Benton brings a wealth of Biblical wisdom, as well as a great deal of sound common sense to this subject. God's unchanging Word is applied skillfully to the issues which challenge us as parents today. Over the past years I have learned a great deal from Ann's seminars on parenting, and also from her example as a mother. I am delighted that she has written this book, and would commend it warmly, especially to new parents.'

Sharon James,
Author and Conference Speaker

'A welcome and stimulating addition to contemporary literature on Christian parenting. The book is full of biblical wisdom and arranged in six lessons. It is honest, practical, readable and stimulating. Ann's book helps parents to take the long view of parenting. What are we doing? We are growing adults! In taking this approach we are encouraged to look at the consequences of particular practices or strategies all too common today. Christian parents will be challenged and helped by the practical advice on family prayers in lesson six. This book will not give all the answers when it comes to parenting today, but it will give you godly guidance.'

Sheila M. Stephen,
Counsellor and Parenting Trainer

aren't they lovely when they're asleep!

Lessons in unsentimental parenting

Ann Benton

CHRISTIAN FOCUS

ISBN 1-85792-876-8

© Copyright Ann Benton 2003

Published in 2003
Reprinted 2004
by
Christian Focus Publications, Ltd
Geanies House, Fearn, Tain,
Ross-shire, IV20 1TW, Great Britain.

www.christianfocus.com

Cover Design by Alister MacInnes

Printed and bound by
Cox & Wyman, Ltd. Reading, Berkshire

Contents

Introduction   9

Lesson 1: Accept   15
Lesson 2: Beware   27
Lesson 3: Communicate   49
Lesson 4: Discipline   65
Lesson 5: Evaluate   85
Lesson 6: Fear the Lord   101

Conclusion   119

Dedication

This book is affectionately dedicated to Matthew, Tom, Jessica and Owen, who have borne with the foolish and frequently sinful idiosyncrasies of their mother with a commendable amount of grace, patience and cheerfulness.

Semper Reformanda
(Always Being Changed)

Introduction

Before we start...

On the grey January day in 1976 that John and I brought our firstborn home from hospital, we looked at each other and sucked in our breath as the weight of responsibility began to descend. Nothing had prepared us for what was to come: not a degree in developmental psychology nor a number of years teaching. I was a new mother and I wanted to get it right. In those early weeks and months I was inundated with advice, much of it conflicting, from professionals, old-hands or even from novices like myself. Living as we did, in the North of England where people talk to complete strangers on the street, I dreaded the onset of infant wails from within the pram as I walked to the local shops.

'He wants a feed, love'
'Put him on his back'
'He's got too many blankets'
'That's a windy cry'

All this well-meaning and cheerfully delivered advice was uttered with such assuredness, that I became completely confused while any confidence I had drained away. My ineptitude was obviously apparent to the whole world.

So, what am I doing writing a book about parenting? I certainly do not want to undermine the confidence of parents. Nobody, apart from God, knows their own child like its parents and nobody, apart from God, has their child's interests so much at heart. I also do not intend that this book should be a written equivalent of a disinterested stranger giving instant diagnoses at the checkout in Sainsbury's. Parenting is far too complex, that much I know.

Some years ago I was invited to speak on the subject of 'Biblical Motherhood in a Child-Centred Society' and this led me to attempt to get back to first principles, starting from the Maker's instructions. Somewhat to my surprise, people seemed to find the talk I gave helpful and I have repeated the seminar, with minor modifications, many times since. I have no technique to offer and remain deeply suspicious of any book which includes its own testimonials. (Wayne and Sherrill followed the EIEIO strategy and Troy's bedroom is now regularly featured in *Beautiful Homes*.) If you are looking for Lily the Pink's medicinal compound, you will be disappointed.

My main aim in this book is to encourage parents to take responsibility, to examine and evaluate the way they behave, consciously or unconsciously, and where necessary, to make some changes. My authority is not my own experience or practice, but what I find in the word of God. Strangely, experience and practice bears it out! I once gave a couple of seminars on parenting at the local Primary School. Because of the sensitive setting, I omitted all the Bible references but the substance was the same. 'Where do you get all this stuff from?', asked one admiring parent. She was surprised when I told her. But believers will not be surprised. God's perfect law holds true for everybody. His ways may not always be easy; rarely are they instant; but his ways are best.

The structure of this book is simple. It is based around six instructions: accept, beware, communicate, discipline, evaluate and fear the Lord.

Having thus delivered the health warning, let us commence.

Lesson 1

Accept

What is a child? Your answer to that question will determine your attitude and behaviour as a parent. John Gray, the author of the best-selling *Men are from Mars, Women are from Venus* wrote a sequel: *Men are from Mars, Women are from Venus, Children are from Heaven.* His view about childrens' innocence leads him to argue against confrontation and for consultation and adaptation. A view at the other extreme is embodied in Mrs Joe Gargery in Charles Dickens' *Great Expectations.* She brought Pip up 'by hand', which as far as Pip was concerned meant that her hand was laid heavy on him on every possible occasion and he was treated generally with extreme inhumanity.

At the beginning of the twenty-first century, the child is viewed more and more as a commodity or consumer item. For the dual-income, upwardly-mobile, designer-label couple, a child is what they want to get after they have their beautifully furnished home and after they are where they want to be in their careers. Their offspring are almost like fashion accessories, kitted out in the latest stylish clothing and surrounded by state of the art child technology. They expect their children to enhance *their* lives.

So as parents the first thing to do is:

A: Accept the truth about your child.

1. Your child is uniquely created

For you created my inmost being; you knit me together in my mother's womb (Psalm 139:13).

Not only is your child a gift, he or she is hand-made and absolutely unique. One of the charms of being a teacher was to me the fact that I never met the same child twice. This fact lends immense significance to every child regardless of appearance or performance. Each child has intrinsic value because he or she was uniquely created by God. That smile, that agility, that imagination, that sense of humour, that voice, that dexterity, that intellect and so on.

To truly imbibe this principle will keep you from one of the besetting sins of parenthood: comparison. It sneaks up on you within hours of becoming a parent. Wherever mothers and fathers meet and enthusiastically discuss their offspring, comparison is irresistible. Emily is sleeping through the night; Matthew is out of nappies (did it in two days!); Tom has read all the books in the reading scheme; Katie got level 6. The road of comparison never ends and for most parents except those of the unspeakably talented, it is stony. To avoid it, continually remind yourself with thankfulness about the unique and wonderful creation which is your child. That way you can happily allow other parents to do the same about theirs and be very mellow about the success of others.

2. Your child is a sinner

Surely I was sinful at birth, sinful from the time my mother conceived me (Psalm 51:5).

Of course there is an innocence about children. There is so much of which they are not aware and they are trusting of adults in a way which can alarm us. They are vulnerable and deserve the protection of adults. But children also have an in-built bias towards deceit and rebellion, which can manifest itself at quite an early age. This is part of being human. It is common to all the human race and all of human history. It is frequently observed that no one has to teach a child to lie. Once a child realizes that his or her parent cannot see round corners, he or she will exploit this to advantage.

Acceptance of this fact about your child, however endearing and charming his or her ways, will save you from being shocked. It doesn't mean you turn into Mrs Joe and beat him in case he's thinking of doing anything. It means you are wise to his or her capabilities in every sense. It may help you not to panic if you realize that your child's misbehaviour is quite normal.

3.Your child is an arrow into the future.

Like arrows in the hands of a warrior are sons born in one's youth (Psalm 127:4).

Hardly a week goes by without some new revelation about our genetic programming. Sometimes it feels as though the script has already been written, which in a way makes a nonsense of a book like this. The Bible teaches that the parental input is vital and the impact of parental intervention and direction is crucial and far-reaching. Whatever the unique genetic make-up of your child (engineered by God) the parental assignment is to direct. Just that.

Our lives on this earth are temporary and short. Our footprints in the sand are soon washed away. But we have a responsibility to the future of the planet of potentially greater significance than the saving of the rainforest or the preservation of the giant panda. The raising of your children is a specific and personal assignment, which could have huge, even global implications. Adolf Hitler had parents; so did

John Wesley. If you don't take care to direct your arrows carefully, who will? This concept raises the significance of raising children way above the level of making sure they are minded when you are at work or taking them to Disneyland. It needs saying in this generation that family care is a worthwhile life choice and the continued pressure on mothers to combine work and parenthood is unlikely to be in the interests of the nations' children or of the future of our society.

4. Your child has a special place in God's heart.

Jesus said, 'Let the little children come to me, and do not hinder them, for the kingdom of heaven belongs to such as these' (Matt. 19:14).

Most parents are quietly passionate about their children. In those early weeks it is as though that little hand grips your heart and many a moment will be spent in glowing contemplation of this amazing being, yours but not yours, part of you and yet independent. Of course there will be times when this object of such affection causes you deep deep pain, precisely because he or she is so precious. At such times it is good to reflect that your child is even more precious to God than he or she is to you. And fatherhood is something God knows about, with all its worst ramifications. There is great comfort in this, particularly if you know the power of prayer.

But there is also accountability. Because your child is precious to God, there are the most severe warnings attached to those who cause a child to stumble. (Matthew 18:5,6) Handle with care.

Having grasped these four truths about your child, you next need to:

B. Accept the truth about yourself

I. You are a sinner too.

Because we parents are in the business of directing and correcting, it is quite easy to forget this. *All sinners here* should perhaps be written on every front door. We have God-given authority to train our children in the right way, but we are so prone to stumble ourselves. We have made all the mistakes! And our motives are so impure. Where does this truth lead us? It leads us to recognize our need for help. I love the story of Manoah and his wife, the parents of one of the Bible's 'miracle' children, Samson. After they have been supernaturally informed that after years of childlessness, they are to have a son, Manoah prays, '**O Lord, I beg you, let the man of God you sent to us come again to**

22

teach us how to bring up the boy who is to be born. His humble attitude is one we would do well to imitate. Our capacity for getting it wrong is immense. But God is gracious.

2. You have baggage.

However many books on parenting we have read, our basic ideas on parenting will have come from having been on the receiving end of it. What kind of parents were yours? It is helpful to think about the way you were brought up and how that has affected you. A mother and a father bring to parenting potentially extremely divergent attitudes, which may not become apparent until a crisis emerges. Views about punishment or about nutrition or about acceptable behaviour at the table or about bedtimes. Perhaps your parents were so brutally strict you determined in your heart way before you had children that you would never ever lay a finger on a child. Perhaps you believe your parents got it absolutely right in every respect and you must follow their example to the letter. Whatever is the case, it is important and salutary to unpack all this baggage and take a good look at it with your wife or husband, so that you can jointly set your course in the light of Scripture.

3. You are responsible.

If you are a believer, your parenting has a particular purpose. God is seeking godly offspring. (Malachi 2:15) Your parenting is not for your gratification, so that you can bask in the reflected glory of your children's success. Your parenting is part of your living for God. As far as it lies with you therefore you will be more interested in your child's holiness than his or her happiness. You will have a spiritual aim, knowing that ultimately happiness is a bi-product of a walk with God. This does not mean that you put a gun to your child's head to profess conversion. Such behaviour is absolutely contrary to the ways of God. But it does mean that you take seriously the commands of Scripture to instruct and correct along Biblical lines and that you make conscious choices towards those things which have spiritual value as opposed to merely material value. It means also that you seek to be an inspiring role model. And your prayers will reflect your most cherished hope to be able one day to say, like Isaiah: 'Here am I, and the children the Lord has given me. We are signs and symbols in Israel from the Lord Almighty, who dwells on Mount Zion' (Isaiah 8:18).

To think over:
Summarize how you view your child.

How is that affecting your attitude to him/her?

To act upon:
Talk with your husband/wife about your respective parents.
Discuss how that has shaped your view of the ideal parent.

Lesson 2

Beware

The wisdom of the prudent is to give thought to their ways, but the folly of fools is deception. (Proverbs 14:8)

There are no techniques in parenting, but there are plenty of pitfalls. As parents, John and I owe a huge debt to John MacArthur Jr who alerted us to some of the pitfalls via a tape we listened to in the early 1980s. Since that time I have reflected and observed and expanded and adapted the original list.

I have never met a parent who did not love his or her child. But, flawed as we are, love is not sufficient to prevent us making misjudgments. Sometimes it is misguided love which leads us into a pitfall and we find ourselves behaving as parents in ways which are not, on reflection, in the best long-term interests of the child. So this chapter is an alphabet of common parental pitfalls, from A – I. As you read and perhaps somewhere see yourself, don't panic. There is time to change. I have fallen into most of these at some time. The danger is when any of these pitfalls become the habitual style of managing your children. There could be sad and serious consequences, as I intend to point out.

A is for Allow-anything

We have all met the child who is allowed to do precisely as she likes. She is never confronted or challenged; rather her parents clear up after her and fall in with her every wish. This can be due to laziness but is more commonly the result of an unwillingness to confront through fear.

a) 'He won't love me'. Fear not. The sad truth is that even children who are most infamously abused by their parents continue to love their parents. They know nothing else. Of course you may win the temporary gratification of a beaming smile by saying 'yes' to everything and you may avoid the appalling scene which embarrasses you in front of your friends, but as parents you are called upon to take the unselfish and long-term view.

b) 'I don't have the right'. I have actually met parents who seriously believe that. They are victims of an iniquitous children's rights propaganda campaign, the underlying philosophy of which is to totally undermine the place of parents and family life. The Bible will have none of it. Enshrined in the fifth commandment is the idea that parents not only have the right but the responsibility to set boundaries for their children.

But does this allow-anything attitude do any harm? Yes it does. Ask any primary school teacher. Such children are frequently extremely insecure. They have been burdened with a freedom which is too big for them. They are also poor listeners and their learning capacity is handicapped. The Bible states the consequences even more seriously. What was God's verdict on Eli's family?

> *For I told Him that I would judge his family for ever because of the sin he knew about; his sons made themselves contemptible and he failed to restrain them* (I Samuel 3:13).

On a more prosaic note, we had written up on the wall of our staircase at home the following text to re-assure me as I ascended the stairs with one of our offspring for a spot of chastisement:

> *The rod of correction imparts wisdom, but a child left to himself disgraces his mother.*

Love them enough to correct them.

B is for Bribery

I am aware that I am about to be somewhat controversial. When I give talks on parenting I have more questions on this point than any other, because it goes against some current thinking on behaviour modification. So first of all, let me explain what I mean by bribery. I mean the operation of a reward system for motivating the child or eliciting from the child some desired behaviour. Here are some examples;

A boy is promised a new play station if he will clean his teeth properly night and morning.

A toddler is promised a packet of sweets if she doesn't scream while she is pushed round the supermarket.

A child gets a sticker on a chart if he goes a whole day without being rude to his parents. (Ten stickers means a trip to McDonalds)

A girl is given pocket money for helping with the drying up.

Those are all real examples. I could give countless more. Make no mistake, it is extremely tempting to go down this road and in the short-term reward systems are highly effective. When I have run Holiday Bible Clubs at church, I have unashamedly used team point systems for crowd control. But that after all is a 4-day event in which there is little opportunity to get to know individual children. As parents, we are not about making our lives easier, we are about growing people. Here are some of the problems with reward systems:

a) The long term impact is minimal. This has been proved time and time again, for example with the teaching of spellings. In the short term, the group who were 'bribed' to learn their spellings achieved better results in the test, but just a few weeks later, when tested on the same spellings there was no difference between the bribed and the unbribed group.

b) If used habitually and continually, extrinsic reward systems produce an unmotivated child – a child who will do just enough to hit off the reward, *and no more*. I will come clean here. We used a ticks on chart system with our own children for a short time until I realized how unhelpful it was. It included things like music practice. So my son went to his room, got out his violin, scraped away about a dozen notes and then shouted, 'Is that enough, Mum?' What was I to answer? Was I to suggest that he had to play at least thirty notes to merit a tick, or was I to do it by the clock. The point is it was not a system to make a musician of him. Just doing enough is not it!

c) It makes behaviour seem negotiable. What if a child decides he doesn't care for McDonalds anymore and would prefer the freedom to be rude, or the girl wants a raise in pocket money or she downs the tea-towel. Beware of taking behaviour and attitudes out of the moral dimension.

Children, obey your parents in the Lord, for this is right (Ephesians 6:1).

Note: they are to obey because it is right, not because of some instant material reward.

Try and think about the kind of person you would want your child to be as an adult. In the list of attributes, would not the idea of self-motivation be included. Or would you want a son or daughter who always calculated what there was in anything for him or her? How much better to train your child from the earliest years to take pleasure from choosing what is good and right.

This does not mean of course that you never give your children treats. There may be occasions when you are aware of how co-operative/patient/ helpful/ cheerful they have been and may say, 'I've really appreciated your attitude today and

I've brought buns for tea to celebrate.' But avoid a system of buns for behaviour.

Love them enough to take the long-term view.

C is for Child-centred

This is very common and in some senses very easy to fall into quite unconsciously. When you bring that scrap in a shawl home from the hospital, your lives are turned upside down. The whole house is ordered for a while around the feeding, changing, bathing, pacifying and (we hope) sleeping of that infant. But having made necessary adjustments to the new member and your new role, it takes a determined effort to organize your lives so that the whole family does not become a victim of one member.

Later on, you will be naturally very keen for your child to have the best of everything and to prosper. Affluent parents are most in danger here. In Surrey there is the common sight of the mother at the wheel of her enormous para-military people carrier. Her whole life revolves around delivering and collecting her children to and from, not just school, but ballet, cubs, brownies, karate, swimming, tennis, orchestra, trampolining, friends' sleepovers etc. etc. At home, great attention is given by everybody to the child's homework. They ought to award GCSEs to parents.

What is wrong with this?

a) You are raising a child who will think he or she is the centre of the universe and one who expects to be provided with diverting and exciting activities from breakfast until bedtime. The worst reproach this child can utter to his or her parents is 'I'm bored.' This generally has the effect of making the said parents spend more money and time or feel that guilty about their apparent failure as parents. Wherever did a child get the idea that life would never be boring, or if it was, it was somebody else's responsibility to make it more interesting? To go far down the road of child-centredness is to raise a selfish brat.

b) You might be jeopardizing your marriage, or even using the child as a prop to support a failing marriage. But remember the creation ordinance of family life puts the priority on the husband and wife relationship.

For this reason a man will leave his father and mother and be united to his wife, and they will become one flesh (Genesis 2:24).

Make sure your marriage relationship continues to thrive after the arrival of children. One way of doing this is to cultivate from an early age the idea of what we call 'healthy neglect'. In other words, build into the day some time when the child is left to his or her own devices, doing something of his or her own choosing or even doing nothing. Children spend far too little time lying on the grass staring at the sky these days. They might learn something (Psalm 8:3,4).

Love them enough to avoid making them the centre of your life.

D is for Distant

Readers of this book are by definition less likely to be guilty of this. But it happens in the best of circles. Perhaps a parent is extremely busy or absorbed in his or her job, or with work in the church, or with a hobby or with other relationships.

A classic example of this kind of parent is Mrs Jellaby in Dickens' *Bleak House*. She has what Dickens describes as 'telescopic philanthropy' – she can see nothing nearer than Africa. Meanwhile her children are tumbling around the house in a state of utter neglect.

A more recent fictional example formed a poignant moment in the film *Dead Poet's Society* which tells the story of events in an upper class boys boarding school in the 1960s. On his birthday a pupil receives by post the present of a desk set from his parents. He looks downcast and his friend asks him why. It is not just that it is not a very exciting or imaginitive present. It is that they sent him exactly the same thing last birthday. The boy realizes that although his parents are extremely ambitious for him to achieve great things they have not taken time or trouble to know him.

The consequence of distant parenting is an angry child. Perhaps it is more commonly fathers who fall into this. For the Scripture warns:

Fathers do not exasperate your children; instead, bring them up in the training and instruction of the Lord (Ephesians 6:4).

Children need fathers as well as mothers and they need fathers and mothers who are 'hands-on'.

Love them enough to get involved.

E is for Explosive

This is a bit like the allow-anything parent but with fireworks. What happens is that finally Mum has had enough. It might be some small thing that is the trigger, like a squabble between the children about which TV channel to watch. But the momentum has been gathering with the mayhem, and suddenly she goes berserk. She throws the TV remote out of the window, bundles the children, with accompanying swipes at various parts of their anatomies to their rooms and shouts in a voice to be heard at the end of the road that they had better go to bed now as supper is cancelled. An extreme example but most parents of young children admit to more than an occasional explosion. Parenting , especially the full-time variety in the early years is hard and sometimes tiresome work. A house full of sinners is a house under some strain. But there is a danger that exploding, because of its immediate devastating impact, could become the way you manage behaviour.

What's wrong with that?

a) Child A to child B: 'It's all right. We can carry on until she really starts shouting'

b) A child becomes anxious – always worrying about the effect of his or her behaviour on you, instead of just doing the right thing.

c) Such a lack of self-control may lead you to do or say harmful things, which you may later regret.

A quick-tempered man does foolish things (Proverbs 14:17).

d) It is an appalling example to your children of how to behave when things don't go your way.

Do not make friends with a hot-tempered man, do not associate with one easily angered, or you may learn his ways... (Proverbs 22:24,25).

The way to avoid this pitfall is to be a thermostat not a thermometer. A thermometer rises with the temperature. A thermostat is set to prevent the temperature rising beyond an optimum temperature. So early intervention is the answer. Defuse the bomb before it explodes. Use distraction, quiet correction or time-out and so avoid an unpleasant explosion.

Love them enough to be proactive.

F is for Fault-finding

Of course children need appropriate correction. But the pitfall here is one that a parent falls into when he or she is too busy looking at what other people's children are doing or not doing. This kind of parent cares very much, too much, about what other parents think of him or her. The children have to be the best. When unfavourable comparisons are made, these parents are very critical of their children. They continually pick up on faults in detail. And their concern is more for outward behaviour than inner attitude. Where they should be as parents discussing together the reason for any revealed problem and long-term strategies for dealing with it, they instead focus on the way it all looks and nag the children about their apparent shortcomings.

The result of this sustained criticism will be a discouraged child who lacks confidence. Children thrive in an ethos of praise. The apostle Paul models his behaviour as a pastor on a beautiful picture of family life.

We were gentle among you, like a mother caring for her little children
(I Thessalonians 2:7).

We dealt with each of you as a father deals with his own children, encouraging, comforting and urging you to live lives worthy of God...
(I Thessalonians 2:11,12).

Love them enough to encourage them.

G is for Guilty

Many parents tell me that they feel permanently guilty. In some cases this is because they are going against what they know to be right – perhaps they are both too career driven and the children seem to be suffering. That sort of guilt is good for us. It is meant to make us re-assess our priorities and change our behaviour.

But some parents are aware that due to circumstances *beyond their control* they cannot provide for their children as they would have liked. A lone parent might feel deeply for the child's loss and feel responsible even where that is not the case. The temptation then is to try to make amends to the child in ways which are inappropriate. I have often observed that financially hard-pressed parents spend a disproportionate amount of their meagre income on their childrens' clothes and birthday presents. It is generally the middle class parents who are most comfortable with hand-me-downs. (Things that come in a bag, as my daughter used to call them).

All that is understandable but there is a danger that a child will catch on to a parent's guilt and become extremely manipulative. He or she will find that all sorts of treats and goodies can be wangled out of Mum or Dad by playing the 'poor me, I'm a victim' card. We do our children no favours when we allow them to see themselves as victims. Everything depends on the correct response, as James points out to his readers when writing about their attitude to trouble.

> *When tempted, no-one should say, 'God is tempting me.' For God cannot be tempted by evil, nor does he tempt anyone; but each one is tempted when, by his own evil desire, he is dragged away and enticed* (James 1:13,14).

The answer to guilt is confession and forgiveness. These should be directed to God in the first place (1 John 1:9) and to the child where appropriate. To admit to your child if it is the truth that you have been woefully busy and have spent too little time with him and to ask his forgiveness might be a salutary lesson in honesty and an opportunity for a child to learn about forgiveness from an unaccustomed end. Children are very forgiving of their parents. But avoid any suggestion of litigious claims for compensation. They don't need that.

Through love and faithfulness sin is atoned for; through the fear of the Lord a man avoids evil (Proverbs 16:6).

Love your children enough to keep short accounts.

H is for Hedging

This occurs where a child is parent-controlled to such an extent that independent behaviour is a very rare experience. Again it is driven by fear, knowing:

a) that the child being a terrible sinner will get up to all sorts of mischief and that the answer therefore is to keep him or her on a very short rein. So the child's day is strictly timetabled to minimize opportunities for anti-social or challenging behaviour. So after school there is a drink, followed by 15 minutes television followed by 30 minutes reading, followed by 20 minutes piano practice, followed by tea, followed by bathtime etc. etc. The holidays are planned similarly. Everything is organised to the last minute.

b) That the world is a dangerous place and you cannot ever let your child out in it alone. In fact it is far preferable to buy him toys and encourage activities which keep him where you can see him. Television watching is ideal.

A child brought up where this is the predominant parental thought will not have the opportunity to use independence well. These children are the worst behaved children in the Sunday School, unless of course one of their parents is teaching. As soon as they realize that the parents are not around, they are up for any kind of misbehaviour going. It is their only opportunity. These children would have learnt far more by being given the freedom to fail. As it is they have learnt to be deceitful and furtive.

I have a great deal of sympathy for the parent who is driven by the fears outlined in (b) above. The world is physically far more threatening than a generation ago. For children who grow up in towns and cities, playing football or hopscotch or cycling in the street, as their parents probably did, is impossible. And then there is the stranger danger which is perceived to be greater than ever. But there are dangers indoors too and the box in the corner of the sitting room is amongst the most pernicious. There has also been expressed right and serious concern about the lack of exercise most children get. Parents must arrange and allow and encourage children to get off their backsides and as appropriate to their stage of development they must be allowed to do things independently even though there may be a slight risk attached. So to run an errand to the local shop is a suitable task for a child, once the parent is satisfied that the varying hazards can be safely negotiated. This is as important a part of their education as the learning of their tables.

Love them enough to let them go.

I is for Inconsistent

In some ways this is the most dangerous of all the pitfalls and it has various manifestations

a) This kind of parent is more interested in the effect of a child's behaviour on him or herself, so that what is a capital offence one day because of your mood or because you are in public is ignored the next day. When the pastor comes to tea the children come in for a load of discipline but the next day it doesn't matter.

b) Inconsistency is also seen when foolish threats are made which even a child knows will not be carried out. 'If you do that again, I'll kill you' is an extreme example but a threatened withdrawal of a privilege can be just as foolish, especially if the bouncy castle is already booked. Children will call your bluff.

c) Inconsistency in policy between mother and father is an invitation for children to play one off against the other.

d) Favouritism of one sibling over another is mean and stores up ghastly consequences for the future. Remember Joseph and his brothers. (Genesis 37)

The outcome of inconsistent parenting is an unruly child, which means that the job of parenting gets progressively harder with years and not easier. With inconsistent parenting, children learn that adults do not mean what they say, or if they mean it today they won't tomorrow. Instead there must be training, a word which implies continuance, patience, persistence and clear guidelines, consistently applied.

Train a child in the way he should go, and when he is old he will not turn from it (Proverbs 22:6).

Love them enough to mean what you say.

To think over:
Which of pitfalls A – I are you most frequently
falling into?

Why do you think that is?

To act upon:
List some ideas that will help you avoid this in
the future.

Lesson 3

Communicate

Whenever I have a conversation with a fellow parent about rearing children, or whenever I speak at a meeting on the subject, there is one question in the minds of the listeners:

'How do I get him or her to behave?' They want me to talk about discipline. But I have to remind them about the cart and the horse. Or about the fact that a farmer would be foolish to look for a harvest if he had not done any sowing.

Discipline that is worthy of the name cannot happen in a vacuum. Of course you can set up your household with rules and regulations and insist on obedience. But there is a true saying which bears repeating: *Rules without relationship lead to rebellion.*

Think about Captain Von Trapp in the film *The Sound of Music.* His seven children lived by his whistle; they were drilled. He thought his household was entirely shipshape and was blind to the fact that his eldest daughter was seeing an unsuitable young man, while the rest of his children, although apparently submissive were actually subversive. Maria, the governess, is bold enough to eventually confront him with the fact that he doesn't *know* his children. He doesn't play with them, he doesn't meet them where they are.

All the early studies on child-rearing confirmed that the most effective behaviour

management stemmed from firmness **in the
context of a warm relationship.**

Consider this triad:

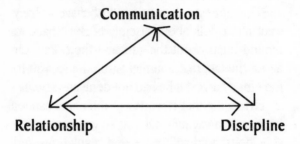

Communication

Relationship   **Discipline**

These three are integrally linked. Note that the
arrows go both ways: one feeds on another. So
not only is discipline more effective where there
is a warm relationship, but a relationship is
actually enhanced by good discipline. After all,
no one likes the company of an unruly child for
long. And contrary to what you might expect,
children do not love their parents less for being
firm and consistent. They generally are all the
more concerned to win your approval and are
therefore at their most endearing. So, everybody
wins.

But the other corner of the triad is no less
important. Discipline improves communication
because everybody is reminded of the boundaries
and of who is in charge. Discipline also requires

communication and the better the communication, the easier it will become.

Communication is also vital to a positive relationship; you might call it foundational. But again, the best relationships foster the keenest communication. The people you are closest to understand you best and vice versa. You can communicate quite explicitly with someone who knows you well with the raise of one eyebrow.

So let's think through the nature of communication.

a) Watch your language.

Truth and love. The Bible says you must have both (Ephesians 4:15). And that what comes out of your mouth should be helpful (Ephesians 4:29). Words can build up or they can crush. Those who are proud of the fact that they call a spade a spade are often oblivious to the damage that a spade can do to tender plants. On the other hand, there is an equivalent danger of being the kind of parent who always strokes and smoothes and fails to correct (See A is for Allow anything in Lesson 2.) Truth and love must go hand in hand in all your communication so make a very careful bridge with your words, knowing their power to wound.

Tone of voice. From an early age, before an infant understands the words that you say, he or she will learn to recognize your intent from your intonation. A harsh shout directed at someone else will make the baby cry. On the other hand the soft and gentle tongue can achieve an entrance, win friends and influence people.

A gentle answer turns away wrath, but a harsh word stirs up anger (Proverbs 15:1).

Through patience a ruler can be persuaded, and a gentle tongue can break a bone (Proverbs 25:15).

Body language. *You say it best when you say nothing at all,* was the refrain of a recent popular song. How do you best communicate to your child your interest in him and his world? By smiles and looks, by stopping what you are doing and turning to face him, by listening, nodding. All without speech. And how do you communicate to a child the cruel reverse of that? By the newspaper kept up in front of your face, by the walking away, by the preoccupied stare into space, while she rattles on.

Other messages can be easily and effectively communicated without words. Picture the frown which says, 'That is inappropriate behaviour', or the smile which says, 'You are very special to me.'

b) Learn (and teach) to listen.

He who answers before listening – that is his folly and his shame (Proverbs 18:13).

Four components. In order for real communication to take place, four things have to happen: A speaks, B listens, B speaks, A listens. It is very easy to think that communication is about getting your point across, or about everyone having his say. It tends to be the listening components which are neglected but James reminds us that we should all be quick to listen but slow to speak (James 1:19).

Listening must be learned (by you). As the adult member of the partnership you have to be prepared to take the trouble to listen. When a child is learning to talk, it takes the enthusiastic expert, i.e. you, the proud parent, to interpret it back. Other listeners may be completely mystified by the infant utterances, but you know. And your automatic response to listen, interpret and repeat it back, perhaps more precisely, is not only excellent for the child's growing grasp of language but is a perfect lesson in communication. Sadly, when children learn to articulate more clearly, parents stop doing this, forgetting that though speech is well advanced, language and the ability to express a feeling is still in its infancy. So, not only has the parent to listen to the words but to search for the emotion behind the words. For example a child who says, 'I'm hopeless at reading' is not looking for an argument about the facts concerning his own achievements in literacy or whether he is better or worse than anyone else, or a lecture of the 'no gains without pains' variety. He is expressing his discouragement. The wise parent reads that message and looks for opportunities to build confidence and self-esteem, including possibly the tackling of a well-known and much loved text next time they read together.

Listening must be taught. In a televisual age, a child can lose the ability to pick up cues merely from listening. He or she learns to rely on visual cues for understanding. Teachers in reception classes find that many children cannot follow a simple spoken instruction, not because they are rebellious but because they do not have the necessary skills to hear words and decode them into a spur for action on their part. No wonder the so-called attention deficiency disorder (ADD) is on the increase. Nobody had ever heard of it before the widespread and continual infantile pastime of watching TV and video. I am not advocating the outright prohibition of television watching for children, but parents who allow their children that pleasure must be careful that their children do not lose the ability to learn by listening. Here are some ways in which you can encourage good listening skills.

• *Tell* stories. That is to say, instead of sharing a book with your child and reading the text, occasionally just get eyeball to eyeball contact and tell the story. Stop and ask questions occasionally, e.g what do you think happened next?

• Play listening games. Simon Says is a classic example. But there are many. Games which include lists like 'I went to the moon and found a ....' are good for training memory and listening. A ridiculous favourite with my children was the one called 'I'll do one thing while you do another' in which we gave each other crazy instructions and added to them, e.g. Stand on one leg; stand on one leg with a cushion on your head; stand on one leg with a cushion on your head and a finger in one ear; etc. etc. until someone falls over laughing.

• Give instructions and messages. This is a good way to assess progress in listening. Can your child reliably repeat a message from you in the bedroom to Daddy in the kitchen. Give them practice. Give instructions and monitor the ability to carry it out. Very small children can only cope with one instruction at a time but as they grow, encourage the ability to receive and carry out two, then three, then four or five given instructions. Set it as a challenge.

c) Make the relationship.

You say, we have a relationship, my children and me. Of course you do. But it will stand a little scrutiny and the investment of some time for consideration. Do not take that relationship for granted. Parent/child relationships can wither and die for lack of attention. In most cases the parents concerned did not want that to happen. But not wanting it to happen is not enough. On several occasions a parent has admitted wistfully to me, 'It was great when they were little; we used to have such fun as a family.' But as teenagers these same children have firmly closed the door and there is in the house an atmosphere of tension and resentment. Parents who take particular joy in playing with their children when they are little, need to be prepared to adjust to the growing child's development. There are periods of rapid growth, both physically and emotionally. Your relationship must be elastic enough to take that strain and hang in there.

That is one reason why I sub-titled this book, *Lessons in unsentimental parenting*. Our love for our children must not be tied up with their cuteness. They don't stay cute. They get smelly, spotty, awkward, secretive and rude. They are not less precious then. Another title I toyed with was '*Feeding the mouth that bites*', because that is what parenting can feel like. It takes a lifetime of conscious commitment to *make* the relationship.

There are three myths about building relationships that I would like to explode:

The myth of quality time. With children you have to think quantity, not quality. The quality of any time you spend with them will only be recognized with hindsight. So it won't do to plan in your diary the first Friday in the month for an evening of quality time with the children. By all means plan to spend time with them, but don't be disappointed if they reject your attempts to impress them with your undivided attention. They may not need it that night. They might need it another night when it will not be to your convenience because you are having an early night, dog-tired after a long day. But you will put on your dressing gown and sit on your daughter's bed and hear her heartaches and you will be glad to have been there for her. That will only happen if you have been around for the humdrum times too. If there has been such a thing as quality time in our family life it has generally been around the meal table on ordinary days. This is a daily practice which I would encourage you to move heaven and earth to follow. It is a dying tradition in Britain in these days. Children eat alone or on the sofa in front of the television or in front of the fridge or up in their bedrooms. Not only is this a bad idea for their nutritional habits, it is huge loss to their education and training in its broadest and best possible sense. It is at the meal table that current events can be discussed, the significant or trivial events of the day shared, laughed, cried or prayed over. It is at the family table that family catchphrases are born, the silliest of songs sung, and memories are recounted and turned into family legend. Not only so, but what an opportunity for input. Moses told the Israelite people to talk to their children about the things that really mattered, not in the formal setting of a schoolroom, but:

> *Talk about them when you sit at home and when you walk along the road, when you lie down and when you get up* (Deuteronomy 6:7).

In other words, whenever. That's quality time.

The myth of things. Does life consist in the things that we possess? I hope I hear a resounding 'No!' (Luke 12:15). Then why do we as parents give credence to the materialist lie by overloading our children with things? The answer is that we get great pleasure from giving to our children. To buy a toy for our child is more fun than buying something for ourselves, not least because the child in us is going to enjoy playing with it too. But we need to exercise caution. If we overload our children with things we will diminish for them the thrill of receiving. We will rob them of joy. And we will raise in them expectations about what is their due and the source of their joy. I heard a very sad story about some delightful people who always were pleased to express their love for their children by buying lavish presents for them. Imagine their horror when one Christmas day, their eleven year old son opened his not inconsiderable gift and looked up and said with a frown, 'Is this it?' The point is that although there may occasionally be precious things you give your children which they will treasure for their lifetimes, most presents will not be in that category at all. On a humble, practical note, I always attempted when choosing a gift for one of our children to take it down one notch from my original idea. So instead of the Lego Super-Duper Set, I would get the Super one. They never knew. Most often they liked the box better anyway. Presents do not enhance relationships in the long-term. More than any material gift, what your children will remember and treasure all their lives are the times you had together, your collective adventures and escapades, the funny things that happened, the magic moments. So put your wallet away and build a bank of memories.

The myth of 'educational'. Parents are genuinely and rightly concerned that their children learn and this concern is often reflected in the choices they make of toys, TV programmes or outings. Don't get me wrong: discernment is crucial as I shall underline in a later lesson. But we can have too narrow a view of educational. Museums are fascinating places and these days many are very child-friendly and an excellent day out but we don't always have to look for that kind of input. A game of cricket in the field next to the campsite might be no less valuable. Keen parents need to be encouraged to chill out and lighten up from time to time.

A cheerful heart is good medicine, but a crushed spirit dries up the bones (Proverbs 17:22).

Remember the principle of healthy neglect. Allow time for doing nothing around each other. Or do wild things. Physical games which involve a good deal of chasing, shrieking and rolling around are important for young children, especially boys. Imaginitive role-playing games, from cowboys and Indians to doctors and nurses, are equally precious. Play with them on their terms. Enter their worlds. Surprise them. They won't forget it. It will be a cherished memory – the day Mum and Dad dressed up as pirates at the tea table. All your lives are enriched in the investment of your time into making the relationship.

To think over:
Which of the four components of real communication is weakest in your interaction with your child?

To act upon:
What steps will you take to improve it?

List here some activities which have enhanced or could enhance your relationship with your child.

Lesson 4

Discipline

The children's rights lobby has been, in the last two decades, loud and vocal. The motivation and source of this lobby and the 'evidence' it purports to bring are in fact deeply suspect, as Lynette Burrows in her excellent book *Fight for the Family* has demonstrated. However, to protect children from abuse at home is obviously the duty of every right-thinking person. And many such parents have been swayed by the argument that it is an abuse of a child per se to discipline, correct and punish a child. Aside from the difficulties that brings to parents on a daily basis and the long-term consequences suffered by teachers and society at large, this argument is quite the reverse of Scripture teaching. The Bible says again and again that correction and discipline are *good* for children. They are the acts of a loving parent after the pattern of the loving Father God who disciplines *his* children. More than that, it is an act of the utmost cruelty to withhold discipline from a child. It would be like allowing your children to play on a railway line. A recent court case in Wales found parents who did just that guilty of manslaughter. But take note:

> *Do not withhold discipline from a child; if you punish him with the rod, he will not die. Punish him with the rod and save his soul from death* (Proverbs 23:13,14).

In other words discipline is for the child's sake and the child's safety. Amy Carmichael was taught as a young child to thank her father after chastisement, as an acknowledgement of this fact. It is important to get this clear at the outset of a chapter on discipline. The point of discipline is not for your own quiet life or convenience or as an outlet for your anger. It is the equivalent of teaching a child to swim, i.e. necessary for safety.

Discipline however is not the same thing as punishment, though it may undoubtedly include that. Discipline is a planned strategy for training by means of instruction, encouragement, correction, modelling and the imposition of sanctions.

It is crucial to remind ourselves also that Biblical discipline always gives priority to the inner before the outer. *That you may gain a heart of wisdom* is the stated aim of the book of Proverbs. Attitude is everything. Too often as parents we are concerned with the outward – clothes, appearance, achievements in school tests. If these are OK we are satisfied. But it is quite possible for a child who excels in all these points to be proud, worldly, deceitful, selfish or even lazy. Yet such sins are far more serious than a liking for modern apparel, untidiness or an inaptitude for academic work, which of course is not a sin at all. But many parents even unconsciously give the message that outward appearance and achievements at school are everything.

Why do children misbehave?

There is the theological answer to this question, of course. They misbehave because they are, as we all are by nature, rebellious sinners. Let us look at the question from a simple psychological perspective. There are five main reasons why children misbehave:

a) to get attention.

From the earliest age an infant learns that it works like nothing else. Children crave attention from their parents and if they can't get it one way they will get it another. So they find it amusing to keep opening the forbidden cupboard while you are talking on the telephone. Of course you have to correct this kind of misbehaviour but you also have to attempt to break the child of using this means to get your attention. So the rule is *Catch them being good*; and when you do your attention and praise will teach them that this is the better way. It can be quite hard on some days to catch your toddler being good. But work at it. This is such effective training because it strengthens your relationship with the child even while you are explicitly stating what kind of behaviour or attitude meets your approval. And all this is done without shouting or tears. Everyone thrives in an ethos of praise. The accepted wisdom is that the ideal atmosphere for learning is for praise to outweigh correction by about 3:1, but that if you want to initiate new or a complete change of behaviour praise should outweigh correction 10:1.

b) to challenge authority.

This is the big one, which has the hallmark of sin indelibly upon it. The subtle thing about it is that this kind of misbehaviour manifests itself as often in small things like the curled lip, the slammed door, the muttering under the breath as in the more obvious acts of defiance or rank disobedience. This type of misbehaviour must be corrected very firmly and clearly. Set or restate the boundaries and do not flinch. It does not matter if your child goes to bed thinking that Mummy or Daddy is being a bit grim. It is important that your child goes to bed knowing who is in charge. Remember that God has given you this authority and while you are not to abuse it you are certainly to exercise it. For this you will be held to account.

c) to hurt.

Yes, sometimes even to hurt you, the beloved parent. Because you are there and because they can trust you to still love them and because they are angry or frustrated after a trying day at school, they will be rude or objectionable at home. Again this must be corrected, but gently, being careful to deal with the issue itself. Because you are wounded or inconvenienced by this behaviour you will be tempted to retaliate in a 'you've spoiled my day, I'll spoil yours' kind of mood. Put that away. You are the grown-up here, remember? On the other hand, do not make too many excuses for your child or you rob them of the right to take responsibility for their own behaviour. I have sometimes heard young children on the point of chastisement, bleating 'I'm tired'. They do that because they have heard so many times their parents making this excuse for them to others, as though that makes bad behaviour OK. The child may indeed be tired and the wise parent will make arrangements for less activity and more sleep in the very near future but even a young child must learn that to be rude or disobedient is the wrong way to handle tiredness. Don't inculcate the victim syndrome in your child. You do him or her a huge disservice.

d) to win friends' approval.

I remember my two older boys, aged three and four, having friends to play. They were quite well aware of what was and was not done vis-à-vis furniture and toys in the bedroom. My horror on entering the bedroom after leaving them to entertain their friends for a short while, I still recall to this day. My normally well-behaved and compliant children had pulled the mattresses off the bunkbeds, removed every book from the shelves, turned out every drawer and emptied every box of toys. It was a work of utter demolition and they and their friends were full of glee, until they saw my face, that is. What had caused them to do this? It was an early manifestation of peer pressure. They wanted to impress their friends with a show of bravado. So there was work to be done by me the parent after they had been made to clear up the mess. That work is a long-term and serious work because the child who wrecks his bedroom to impress his friends will be the child who will be afraid to turn down drugs offered to him in some corner of the playground. So children need to be taught the importance of principled behaviour and guided in their choice of friends. See Proverbs 1: 10-19 for Solomon's clear warning to his son along these lines. As children near the critical adolescent phase, peer pressure becomes the dominant force in their lives. James Dobson's *Preparing for Adolescence* remains as helpful a book as ever on this and other subjects and is recommended reading for parents with their pre-adolescent children.

e) to signal inadequacy.

Have you ever witnessed a child misbehaving in a restaurant and felt sympathy with the embarrassed parents' attempts to discipline their child? Have you ever given your child a toy which said on the box, suitable for age eight and over, but because you believe your child to be 'very bright for his age' you gave it to him or her at age five? And then you were cross because they didn't play with it properly. Both those scenarios are cases where a child's misbehaviour is signalling inadequacy. You are asking of the child something he cannot deliver because he is too little or he does not yet have the skills. It happens in schools where a child is given an inappropriate task and then covers her inability to perform it by playing up. That is why a good teacher will frequently differentiate tasks so that children are given work which suits their ability and meets their needs. Parents must also sometimes differentiate. If a child is signalling inadequacy, change the task. Sometimes children are naughty because they are being given too many choices.

Little children do not handle well a wide range of choices. Do not be afraid to be directive.

The parents' responsibility.

The Bible gives one rule to children: obedience to their parents (Exodus 20:12). So obedience is the general expectation which parents are right to have of their children. However, within that general expectation, there will at different times and phases of growth be a particular focus. You will notice as parents a particular area which needs shaping up. Perhaps it may be coming when called, or answering politely, or not interrupting, or not whining, or sharing toys. So particular rules will be engendered with reference to those specific areas. It is probably ill-advised to work on more than two or three areas at a time. Having as parents agreed the way that you are going there are four stages:

a) establish rules – *be realistic*

In Deuteronomy 5:29-33 Moses sets out to the Israelites clearly what the rules are. Parents must do no less to their children. Sometimes, sadly, children only really find out what the rules are by breaking them. In establishing rules the watchword is : *be realistic.* Ask yourselves if the behaviour you are requiring is within the capabilities of your child at this point in their development. As a young inexperienced teacher I caused myself a lot of grief by insisting on certain behaviours which were frankly just too much. I then had all the trouble of policing these things. I had been unrealistic.

b) explain rules – *be clear and fair*
Solomon in Proverbs 1:8-19 explains why he is laying down precepts for his son. It is not just because 'I say so', although you have the authority to do that. Infants of course are not ready for explanations but as children's language and reasoning skills develop it is sometimes helpful to ask a child, 'Why do you think I say that?' or 'Why is that important?' Get them on board and there will be little need for sanctions. Clarity and fairness are essential.

c) enact rules – *be inspiring*
This may not always be possible but it frequently is. For example, if the issue is moaning, install a mental tape-recorder to your own speech. Is there a touch of them in you as you face the challenges of life? If there is, then start addressing that issue in your own life by responding cheerfully, calmly and patiently. Show how it is done. The same applies to many other attitudes and behaviours. Sometimes we will discover that children have learnt some of their

less endearing characteristics from us. So turn that round and be an inspiring role model. The apostle Paul is able to say to the Philippian church:

> **Whatever you have learned or received or heard from me, or seen in me – put it into practice** (Philippians 4:9).

Parents should be able to say 'no' less to their children.

d) enforce rules – *be firm, consistent and self-controlled.*

Rules are enforced through a mixture of training (example, observation, comment, practice), encouragement and punishment. Allow time for learning and gentle correction but be firm and vigilant. Having established the rule one day don't ignore the breach of it the next just because you are feeling a bit tired. This is why it is good to focus on only a few areas at a time.

Punishment, which will be called for where there is outright disobedience of the challenging authority type, may make use of natural consequences, logical consequences or direct action.

Natural consequences are a parent's friend. But too often parents protect their children from them. Don't! It is good for a child to learn that sin has unpleasant consequences. So, if the focus is a lazy or slapdash attitude, and a child forgets his homework and gets in trouble at school, resist the urge to complain to the teacher or rush to your child's defence. Make him or her responsible. If the focus is clearing up toys on the bedroom floor and because it wasn't done, something gets lost or broken, do not rush to replace it or repair it. Make the most of the teaching opportunity.

Logical consequences are of the type much favoured by the Mikado, whose 'object all sublime'…was 'to let the punishment fit the crime.' So, if the focus is punctuality and reliability about meeting time constraints and a young teenager fails to get home on time after being allowed a Saturday afternoon shopping expedition with her friends, then the logical consequence is not to be allowed to go out next Saturday afternoon.

Direct action refers to the imposition of fair sanctions, for the purpose of making the point that disobedience ultimately incurs pain. Whether that pain is inflicted physically, financially, by the removal of privileges, or the removal of the perpetrator to his or her room is absolutely the decision of the parent who will take into account the needs and nature of the child. I am not ashamed to say that I smacked my children. Apart from the fact that it is categorically recommended in the Bible, I found it had many advantages over other sanctions. It is immediate and soon over which is far preferable than the looming type of penalty, which makes the in-between time rather unpleasant atmosphere-wise. Also those long-term sanctions require unrealistic powers of memory on the part of a busy parent. Once the point has been made via a tap or slap, good relations are quickly and in my experience, warmly restored. The incident is over.

The anti-smacking lobby who have managed to make smacking of children under three illegal in Scotland and who will continue their efforts until the same or more is done in the rest of Britain, need to be recognized for what they are, as anti-family. This is not the place to engage with that particular debate. You can endorse their point of view if you like. However, show me a family with grown up children who are well-motivated, self-controlled, cheerful, loving and honest citizens and I will show you a family where the parents were not afraid to smack their young children when they were naughty. My own experience is that the optimum time for smacking is before school age and that if you are unflinching then, you are rarely called upon to use 'the rod' afterwards. It is said that children learn more before they are five than in the rest of their years put together: this is certainly true in the area of self-discipline. My oldest son, at age three and four used to see a look on my face and say hurriedly, 'I smack myself!'. He knew well what was coming. Once he learnt to internalize that realization and control his behaviour, there was no need to smack him at all. Another of my children needed far less physical punishment, being far more eager to please and very sensitive to my displeasure. So children are different. The really important thing for parents to remember in this regard is that the worst kind of discipline is that which is imposed when you yourself have lost your temper. It is then that you are likely to over-react and do something damaging or dangerous, whether the punishment is physical or emotional.

How to handle a behaviour crisis.
Sometimes an incident occurs which requires more than the ordinary correction. At such times a parent can feel very discouraged and think, 'What will be the end of this? Will I be prison visiting a few years from now?' The following sequence of questions, which we borrowed and adapted many years ago from some helpful tapes by John MacArthur Jr, may help you to turn a

behaviour crisis into a learning opportunity. Do not panic. Be thankful that something has happened which will enable you to put your cards clearly on the table. The aim is to teach the child to take responsibility for his or her actions. So when you are calm, sit down with the child, insist on eye to eye contact and begin thus:

Question 1: *What did you do?*

The child will always want to tell you what someone else did. Have none of it. While there is a time for listening to extenuating circumstances, the first thing to establish is what the child actually did. The child must see him or herself a responsible agent, and not first and foremost as a victim. You will be tempted to ask 'why?' but resist in the first instance. When you ask why instead of what, you open the door to blame-shifting. Having said that, be fair and probe until you have a full picture.

Question 2: *Was what you did the right or wrong thing to do?*

This question draws the child into the discipline process and forces him or her to make a moral judgment. If the child trusts you and the situation is calm, a child will usually admit a fault and can be commended for such honesty. With an older child you might even ask why it was wrong. The main point here is to bring in the moral dimension. This is training: behaviour is right or wrong.

Question 3: *How might you have handled it in a better way?*

This enables the child to consider other alternative behaviours. Life's challenges present us with choices as to our response. There is always more than one handle. A failure on one occasion might enable the child to see that x was not a good response but y or even z might be preferable. This is learning for the future. If the child cannot think of any alternatives, suggest some, but don't be too quick to do so. The more that actually comes from the child, the better. As the modern idiom puts it, they will have ownership.

Question 4: *The next time a similar situation arises how will you handle it?*

The child will select one of the alternatives from the answer to question 3. You can talk through he practicalities of that. But again, wait for the child's answer. Don't answer for him or her. The purpose here is to get the child committed to a change of behaviour or attitude – more ownership.

Question 5: *Now, if a similar situation arises and you fail to deal with it in the way you have agreed, what do you think would be a fair punishment for not keeping your promise?*

This is an essential step. It amounts to the drawing up of a contract between you. It enables the child to see the justice of the discipline next time. It also enables the child to see the patience and kindness of the parent. There is no punishment this time. The child has a chance to learn and improve. *But* – the next time it happens it is absolutely essential that the parent carries out the sanction as agreed. Not to do so will damage the parents' credibility and render the whole process impotent. The child will then believe that obedience does not matter.

The great thing about this system is that it gives the parent a handle on a crisis. When this dialogue is carried on in a warm although serious tone, it actually enhances the relationship. Something has been understood and agreed between you. The child knows where he or she stands, the boundaries are clarified, but your commitment to him or her is also underlined. So you move on, better friends than you were before.

To think over:
Recall a recent or typical incidence of your child's misbehaviour and work out which of the five reasons in this section 'why children misbehave' account for it.

What is an appropriate response?

To act upon:
Decide, with your husband/wife what should be the current focus for training each of your children.

Write down how and when you will establish, explain, enact and enforce this focus.

Lesson 5

Evaluate

Your child is a receiver, in the tele-communications sense. He or she from the moment of birth, picks up messages and uses them to interpret and understand the world. Young children become quite expert at picking up messages you do not intend them to receive. We called one of our children 'Radar' because he always knew what was going on even when we had taken pains to classify such information as officially secret. As a young child grows, so the input received comes from a range which is far beyond the parent's control.

Recent decades have seen all sorts of alarmist reactions by parents even to activities which a previous generation thought innocuous, or even beneficial. Children's playgrounds had to be resurfaced, in case a child was foolish enough to jump off the top of a slide. Later on, that thinking was reversed in some places, because to always provide a soft landing might encourage children towards a false sense of security and think it was fine to jump off anywhere from any height.

I read about a Sunday School teacher who had an idea for a game which involved the children sticking Post-it notes to their foreheads. A parent, hearing about it, objected that the Post-its might irritate the children's skin. The game was dropped.

Parents are careful to weigh up the potential dangers to their children almost to the point of paranoia. Concern over the possible side-effects of the MMR jab, even on the basis of minimal and inconclusive evidence, caused thousands of parents to opt out of a public health immunisation scheme which has saved many lives. Many children are not allowed to play in the street or walk to school because of the fear that a paedophile is lurking there. Consequently obesity in children is rising.

Of course, many of these concerns are genuine and parents have to take them seriously. But my aim in this lesson is to encourage parents to spend less energy attempting to protect their children from these most rare eventualities, and more in considering and evaluating the messages and pressures which surround the children, both inside and outside the home. These things are far more likely to 'abduct' or permanently 'damage' your child, than a stranger in a mack or an additive in a chocolate biscuit.

I. The Standard

Against what standard shall we measure the input our children receive?

> *Finally, brothers, whatever is true, whatever is noble, whatever is right, whatever is pure, whatever is lovely, whatever is admirable — if anything is excellent or praiseworthy — think about such things* (Philippians 4:8).

This is a helpful guide as far as your own input goes. So, in your conversation and in the stories you read with your children, the films or television programmes you watch, the leisure activities you plan, aim for the true, the lovely and the worthwhile. This does not mean that all stories must be non-fiction. On the contrary. Truth with a capital T can frequently be best carried on the vehicle of a fictional story. The Lord Jesus knew this when he chose to deliver much of his teaching by parable. Some fantasy stories are truer in this sense than a story which seems to be real, because of a familiar context. So make use of a wide range of stories. Be explicit as you make your choice, because the aim is that you are teaching children to be discerning themselves. So at some stage allow them freedom of choice and then get them to evaluate. This is far more valuable than censoring certain programmes or books out of hand. Tempting though it may be to refuse permission to watch TV or films at all, the end of such a procedure is that children will take to secret watching or reading at a friend's house. Then the opportunity for dialogue is closed. How much more educational to watch a programme with your child so that you can evaluate it together.

This issue comes into sharp focus as children reach adolescence. For an excellent guide to the teenage years, I recommend the excellent *Age of Opportunity* by Paul David Tripp. In the book, Tripp analyses the messages of contemporary culture and examines typical responses. He describes two families: the Smiths and the Joneses. The Smiths have brought up their children according to a philosophy of protection by avoidance. So, they have a long list of taboo activities, which would include modern music, dancing, film, TV, etc. This response is dangerous, because it misses the point that the big source of evil is the human heart – not what goes in but what comes out is evil, said Jesus. Such a response sadly leads to deceptive self-righteousness. It also makes children decidedly and unnecessarily isolated and odd in a way that has nothing to do with the gospel.

The Jones children are quite different from the Smiths. They are into all the latest music, fashion and body-piercing. They have TVs in their rooms and are allowed a good deal of freedom. This response to culture is dangerous because it assumes a moral neutrality about everything and there is no attempt by parents or children to evaluate the message.

As is often the case, the middle way is the one to aim for. That is the way of understanding and interacting with the culture. You can train your children from an early age to ask questions, spot lies and make good choices.

2. The resources.

a) The Christian family. This is, or should be, a place of order, love and respect (Ephesians 5: 22-33) of sincere faith (2 Timothy 1:5) and of training and instruction (Ephesians 6:4).

> *By wisdom a house is built, and through understanding it is established; through knowledge its rooms are filled with rare and beautiful treasures* (Proverbs 23:3-4).

I remember as a young mother visiting the home of a Christian family, whose three children were in their teens. We were invited to join the family in an ordinary weeknight meal. I do not recall what we ate but the atmosphere of that home, the quality of the relationships and the conversation was something that impressed me deeply. These are rare and beautiful treasures. I wanted such an ethos in my home for my family.

To create the kind of home which makes it a place to which your children love to return is not a matter of mere maintenance. These treasures are not sold in IKEA. They come through wisdom, which begins with the fear of the Lord. I discovered that such a home will not be created automatically, it needs an investment of time and trouble.

The wise woman builds her house, but with her own hands the foolish one tears hers down (Proverbs 14:1).

To describe a woman as a home-maker would be tantamount to an insult in these days, and yet that is the job-title to which a wise mother will aspire. For such a mother building her house will be of far more importance than progressing in her career or adding to the family income for the sake of a so called higher standard of living.

This positive Christian family ethos will do more to counter all the materialism, consumerism, secularism, hedonism and all the other isms, which are the prevailing messages of our culture, than all the lectures, curfews and worrying in the world.

There was a film made in the 1990s of Louisa M. Alcott's classic, *Little Women*. The strong visual impression created by the film-makers was of the warm glow that epitomized the March family. The burning heart of that glow was Marmee, a mother of exemplary generosity, industry and wisdom. The home that she created for her girls was so magnetically powerful and attractive that lonely Laurie, the boy next door, hardly cared which of the March girls he married. He just wanted to be part of that family. A Christian family can emanate that kind of inviting glow in this cynical world.

b) The meal table. Of course, this is part of the above, but it is so crucial a part that it merits a section of its own. Have you noticed the references in the New Testament to Jesus eating with people? These occasions signify more than merely feeding an empty stomach. The Pharisees muttered about Jesus :

> *This man welcomes sinners, and eats with them* (Luke15:2).

Eating with a person provides a unique opportunity for intimate and important discourse. Hence, the words of Christ to the Laodicean church:

> *Here I am! I stand at the door and knock. If anyone hears my voice and opens the*

*door, I will come in and eat with him,
and he with me* (Revelation 3:20.).

It is at the daily meal table, that the day's input can be reviewed and ideas discussed. It is here that the skills of questioning the assumptions and spotting the lies of contemporary culture can be honed. On the positive side, things that are noble, pure or admirable can be commended and celebrated. Perhaps from the day's stories there will be examples to follow or to avoid. There will be humour and banter and fun. Make eating together an unquestioned priority.

c) The local church. A child who from its earliest years has been brought along readily to Sunday services and other events in a church where the Bible is central to faith and life, has access to a most remarkable extended family. Here are people who have similar standards to your family but who express them through different personalities. Here is a huge pooling of skills and expertise – people to play with; people to question. Here is an opportunity for wholesome activities led by people you can trust. Here are many people each with his or her own story to tell of God's grace. Here are many role-models.

A child of a Christian family will frequently feel an oddity at school or with other friends. But the church is a place to belong. Here there are other children who have parents like yours. They understand. You can relax. Our own children's lives were all enriched by the friendships they made at church, frequently across age boundaries. So, do all you can to encourage church friendships.

d) The wider church. Some smaller fellowships are limited in their resources. For these, in particular, inter-church events, conferences and holidays provide further valuable opportunities as above. It is good for children to hear the gospel, the same gospel, in another context and from different people. Youth camps often provide sustained opportunities for thinking through and discussing issues with others, as well as for hearing some excellent teaching.

3. The balanced programme.

And Jesus grew in wisdom and stature, and in favour with God and men (Luke 2:52)

It has been said that Jesus Christ was the only truly normal child, in the sense of setting the norm. The answer to the question about how should a child develop is that he or she should grow in wisdom, stature, favour with God and favour with men. That makes four areas for development:

- Wisdom – intellectual development.
- Stature – physical development
- Favour with God – spiritual development
- Favour with man – social development.

Growth in all these areas is important for a rounded human being. As parents, according to our own aptitudes or enthusiasms, we are sometimes in danger of focusing on one area to the neglect of another. So the dad keen on football may give a lot of attention to his son's ball skills, fitness and co-ordination but find no time to read the Bible with his son or teach him to pray. Or, parents might be so keen for a child's spiritual progress that they forget that a child needs to run and jump and play.

Most parents delegate some of the input to a school and are careful and critical in their choice of a school. Rightly so. But we need to remember that children spend about five times more of their waking hours at home than they do at school. So perhaps we should be more conscious of what they are learning at home, especially bearing in mind that children learn most not by being told but by watching us. A child whose parents find immense pleasure in reading is likely to discover that joy for herself.

Individual needs also need to be kept in review. For the sake of balance a naturally academic child, who would sit on his bottom all day looking at a book may need to be forced out to the park. A shy, self-absorbed child needs to be given opportunities to learn social skills. Ideally a parent should monitor a child's progress in the four areas of development so that gaps can be spotted and measures be taken to fill gaps. But generally these things will manifest themselves quite naturally; family life is not a training camp, nor should it be.

Every age will have its appropriate focus. In infancy for example a parent will be looking for and encouraging the development of speech and language. This takes a logical and chronological precedence over reading and writing! However concerned you are about literacy, it will actually proceed much better if your children have first learned to speak, listen and enjoy language.

On the physical side, sex education is irrelevant and meaningless to a five year old, but an important topic for instruction and discussion with an adolescent.

All this is a daunting task. Who is equal to it? Do not worry. Help is at hand.

To think over:

What messages is your child receiving from outside the home?

How do these compare or contrast with the messages from inside the home?

To act upon:

Discuss with your husband/wife each of your children's current needs under the headings:

wisdom

stature

favour with God

favour with man

How will you meet those needs?

Complete this grid:

Child's name	Intellectual Development	Physical Development	Social Development	Spiritual Development

Lesson 6

Fear the Lord

He who fears the Lord has a secure fortress, and for his children it will be a refuge (Proverbs 14:26).

Many people, whatever their personal faith or lack of it, might largely agree with the thrust of the first five lessons in unsentimental parenting. But this is the lesson with which many might take issue. 'Why bring in the religious bit?' they may ask. For surely, some may argue, believers do not have the monopoly on good parenting.

It is certainly true that many parents, without any faith in God, do a good job at raising their children to be secure, happy and decent human beings. Nor does that surprise me. The Bible teaches the doctrine of common grace, whereby human beings made in the image of God are capable of great kindness and wisdom. Just because we are all thorough sinners, it does not follow that we are all as bad as we could be. That too is the grace of God.

Nevertheless, it has to be said that the principles outlined in this book are firmly rooted in the Bible. If they find acceptance outside believing circles, that is because present day parents in the western world are still living on the legacy of a culture where the Bible was the unquestioned authority on how to live your life.

When I ask parents of young children to compile a list of attributes they would like to see in their children aged, say, twenty-one, there is a good deal of agreement. Words like generous, loving, hard-working, responsible, considerate are used. These are Christian virtues and I challenge any secular humanist to persuade me of the rightness of them without reference to Christian absolutes. In a welfare state and 'benefits culture', why not bring up your child to be lazy and expect hand-outs. The reason is that something within us cries out that that is not the best way to live; it would be a denial of our humanity. We have been made by God and the Maker's instructions cannot be ignored without some discomfort or malfunction.

It should also be underlined that when parents fear the Lord they are giving to their children the greatest possible security. They are building a fortress for their children. None of us knows the future. As parents, our first thought, were we to be struck by a terminal illness, would be 'what will happen to the children?' All the insurance policies in the world will not make up for the absence of you, the loving parent. But when you have lived your lives in the fear of the Lord, seeking to know him and honour him, then you know that beneath your arms which hold your children are the everlasting arms. There is no security like it. It cannot be bought with money.

The fear of the Lord is the beginning of knowledge, but fools despise wisdom and instruction (Proverbs 1:7).

I. So what is the fear of the Lord?

To fear the Lord is first of all to acknowledge his presence and secondly to be in awe of that presence. God is there and our forgetfulness of that fact will not remove him. He is there; this is his world; he knows us and we are accountable to him. This verse in Proverbs is telling us that until we take all that on board we can never truly understand ourselves, our children or our world. In the context of parenting, this has huge significance. Sometimes our children may question our insistence on some aspect of behaviour or attitude. It is not always possible to explain everything logically to a child's satisfaction. You end up in 'because I say so' mode. But the real truth is this. Your child is accountable to you for his or her obedience; meanwhile you are accountable to God for carrying out *his* instructions. This is not a whim or a matter of personal taste. It is a serious and binding mandate from the God who made the universe.

In addition, this verse in Proverbs sets out the basis of all learning. Educationalists have coined a knew word: learnacy, by which they mean the ability to learn. They find that some children don't have it. They can sit in a classroom all day and learn nothing even though the teacher may be excellent. On the other hand, it is observed that some children have learnacy in abundance. These are children who have a quietness of spirit, an inner calm which allows them to listen and receive what is being taught. Such children, possibly without realizing it, have grasped God's order. They know that they are not the centre of the universe. They do not despise wisdom and discipline and they will go far not merely in the academic sense.

So, only the most foolish parents would not want this for their children. But first....

2. Fear the Lord yourself.

As parents, we are quite good at expecting more of our children than we do for ourselves. We have high aspirations for them. Possibly we want them to succeed where we failed precisely because we have tasted the bitterness of that failure. When it comes to spiritual values, the Bible is quite clear about the order. The main prerequisite for teaching your children to love God is to love God yourself.

> *Hear, O Israel: The Lord our God, the Lord is one. Love the Lord your God with all your heart and with all your soul and with all your strength. These commandments that I give you today are to be upon your hearts. Impress them on your children...* (Deuteronomy 6:4-7).

Christian parents desire more than anything that their children will become Christians. They understand fully that this is God's work. No one is born a Christian. You have to be 'born again' through repentance and faith in Jesus Christ. This is God's work. So Christian parents pray most regularly and fervently that God by his Holy Spirit will work in the hearts of their children.

But God lays on Christian parents the responsibility firstly of maintaining their own spiritual lives. When we are careful to ensure that our children do their daily Bible reading, are we equally careful and diligent about our own? Or have the pressures of life and even parenthood itself caused us to put our own spiritual lives on hold, so that we are just going through the motions? This is dangerous, not least because your children will eventually spot the hypocrisy and be inclined to dismiss with great ease any exhortation to trust Christ or to take seriously his teachings.

3. Who is to do the teaching?

For I have chosen him, so that he will direct his children and his household after him to keep the way of the Lord by doing what is right and just, so that the Lord will bring about for Abraham what he has promised him (Genesis 18:19).

Fathers must take responsibility for teaching the things of God to their children. The father, as head of the house sets the direction. That does not mean that he must do all the teaching. Mothers are also to be teachers:

Listen, my son, to your father's instruction and do not forsake your mother's teaching (Proverbs 1:8).

It is not first and foremost the business of the church, Sunday School or any other Christian agency to teach the children. There should be godly instruction at home, even where, as we learnt in the last chapter, these other agencies are seen and used as valuable resources. They are to be seen as back-up and their agenda will be much broader. So from the earliest age set a pattern of allocating time every day for hearing God's word. Paul wrote of Timothy that from infancy he had known the holy Scriptures (2 Timothy 3:15). What an impact that teaching had made, no doubt due to the sincere faith of those who gave it.

I have been reminded of your sincere faith, which first lived in your grandmother Lois and in your mother Eunice and, I am persuaded, now lives in you also (2 Timothy 1:5).

Christian grandparents can also make a significant contribution.

4. What shall I teach?

• Teach the way of salvation. Timothy's mother and grandmother taught the infant Timothy scripture to make him 'wise for salvation'. Sadly, much Christian literature for young children majors on God as creator and the one who loves us as though to talk of sin and the need for rescue were inappropriate.

- Teach the nature of God.

One generation will commend your works to another; they will tell of your mighty acts. They will speak of the glorious splendour of your majesty, and I will meditate on your wonderful works. They will tell of the power of your awesome works, and I will proclaim your great deeds. They will celebrate your abundant goodness and joyfully sing of your righteousness (Psalm 145: 4-7).

So when you tell Bible stories you will draw out of them what they teach about God, his greatness, holiness, power, goodness and love.

- Teach the law of God. The ten commandments not only tell us more about what God is like, they are the best way to live. But remember that in the covenant of grace, the purpose of the law is to expose our sin and send us running to Christ. Children are naturally legalists and in twenty-five years of Sunday School teaching I have frequently met children from Christian homes expressing the sincere view that you can get to heaven by being good.

• Teach prayer. If the disciples, who were adults, could say to the Lord, 'Teach us to pray', how much more do little children need that instruction.

• Teach the elementary truths. Some of these are listed by the writer to the Hebrews in Hebrews 6:1–2. Some of them might not sound elementary at all but must be included in a rounded programme of instruction. So teach about Christ, repentance, faith, baptism, the local church, what happens when someone dies, eternal judgment. In other words, do not shy away from doctrine, saying to yourself, 'I'll just tell the Bible stories'. Teach doctrine through the stories or teach it through a system of questions and answers i.e. a catechism.

• Teach practical moral behaviour. That is what Proverbs is about. It was written specifically for young people and is packed with insights into life and warnings about the consequences of foolish (i.e. godless) behaviour. They are down to earth and colourful, tackling such important subjects as sexual behaviour, alcohol, anger, laziness, greed, kindness, honesty and pride.

5. How shall I teach?

The notion of family prayers might conjure up a picture of the Victorian household gathered in the dining room in respectful stance, while the patriarch intones Scripture and prayers. That is not the picture in Scripture. There is no indication in the Bible that instruction is by osmosis, in other words that by insisting that children of any age sit with a quiet and attentive demeanour while the word of God is preached and prayers are said you have done your duty in bringing them up in the instruction of the Lord. It is the inside that counts in child-rearing, remember. Many an impeccably behaved child has sat on a hard pew Sunday by Sunday, year on year and the only thing learnt was how to look as though he/she is listening when he/she is not. There is no spiritual gain unless the heart and mind are engaged. Of course, children need to learn that there are times for them to sit still, even if what they are hearing is way over their heads. But let us not deceive ourselves about the value of these exercises to the child's spiritual growth. When the mothers brought their children to Jesus, I cannot imagine that he sat them down and preached a sermon at them. Even when this master-teacher spoke to adults, he nearly always used stories and pictures with contemporary relevance to his audience. Nobody accused him of being patronizing or talking down or not having a serious intent. On the contrary, the people hung onto his every word and commented on his authority. If Jesus took such pains to make his teaching accessible and appropriate to his hearers, should we not do the same for our children? So here are some suggestions concerning family prayers.

• Aim for the regular short time. Don't be too ambitious. Three to five minutes with little children sets the pattern and is long enough to make the statement that God is the centre of our home.

• Consider the level and make it interesting and fun. Use the children's toys to add drama to the Bible story. If you are sitting around the table, use the props that are around you.

• Allow time for questions and include personal testimony in your answers. This is frequently the recommended teaching method in Deuteronomy.

In the future, when your son asks you, 'What is the meaning of the stipulations, decrees and laws the Lord our God has commanded you?' tell him: 'We were slaves of Pharaoh in Egypt, but the Lord brought us out of Egypt with a mighty hand (Deuteronomy 6:20–21).

• Vary the material. Work through different books; use tapes or songs; memorize Scripture; tell missionary or church history stories. Always be on the lookout for new materials.

• Be spontaneous. Although your family prayer time will have a system and a plan to it, do not think that your mandate to instruct your children in the things of God is restricted to that few minutes.

These commandments that I give you today are to be upon your hearts. Impress them on your children. Talk about them when you sit at home and when you walk along the road, when you lie down and when you get up (Deuteronomy 6:6–7).

If God and his word come into your conversation naturally at other times of the day in the context of ordinary life, there will be a reality about your faith which will make its own impact. God is the Lord of all our lives. To have a sacred/secular divide is both artificial and unhelpful. Help your children to see that we live all of our lives before God. That is the fear of the Lord.

6. Actions speak louder than words

Keep in mind that your example is more eloquent than your words. In an anti-Christian culture it is tempting to have worldly priorities. Those worldly priorities include the putting of your children first. Important though your children are, certainly more important than money or fame, to make them your idol is to do them and yourselves a great disservice. Not just because they will be in danger of becoming spoilt and unattractive people; not just because you will in the end demand of them what they cannot deliver and may even drive them away from you. To put your children in the place of God is offensive to him and it will deprive you and your children of the blessing that comes from obedience. To put God first may sometimes in the short-term inconvenience your children. I sometimes think about Noah, who

> *When warned about things not seen, in holy fear built an ark to save his family* (Hebrews 11:7).

I am sure at some points it was very tiresome to have a father who was set upon this enormous project.

'Why are you building this ark, Daddy?'

'Because God told me to.'

But that ark saved his family from the flood. The singleness of heart and mind which it must have taken Noah through all those long years of hard work, as he put God and his word first, was to his own family's blessing. We want our families to be saved. So put God first. Your children will not lose out. On the contrary, God's promise to his restored people is:

They will be my people, and I will be their God. I will give them singleness of heart and action, so that they will always fear me for their own good and the good of their children after them (Jeremiah 32:38-39).

To think over:
If your child was asked, 'How important is God in your parents' life?', what do you think would be the answer?

How would they know?

To act upon:
Write down here some ideas for family prayers/ instruction which you can implement in the near future.

Conclusion

The Exquisite Burden

I started this book by stating that there are no magic formulas to guarantee successful parenting, however you define that success. The main reason for this is that although in our parental role we look on ourselves as very much in charge, of course ultimately we are not. A mere momentary reflection on life as we know it will confirm this simple assertion. Two things which are out of our control:

I. The future
Let me be blunt: we do not know for certain that our beloved child will still be alive tomorrow.

Who of you by worrying can add a single hour to his life? **said Jesus** (Matthew 6:27).

If that doesn't make you feel small it should. Length of days is determined by God. We parents are equally impotent in preventing or even foreseeing the storms and traumas that our children may face. When they were little, you put a guard around the gas cooker and purchased plastic plugs to render electric sockets inaccessible to curious toddler fingers, but later you have to accept, however reluctantly, that they may face crises and suffer experiences more ghastly than anything in your experience, and they will face them without you. You may promise, 'I'll always be here for you.' But that is a promise you are not entitled to make. There is only one person who has ever said truly, 'I will never leave you.' (Hebrews 13:5; Joshua 1:5).

What will keep us sane then in the light of all this uncertainty? Only the knowledge that these matters are under the control of the all-wise, loving Creator, who is true to his promises.

2. Your child's response

Your child is not a computer which you can programme to perform in a certain way. Your child is a responsible agent. He or she makes choices, not least about how to respond to the training you have given. For some parents this will mean watching a beloved child spurn them and their values and set off for a distant country, there to squander everything. What can such a parent do but pray and watch for the return, knowing that there is a heavenly Father who knows exactly how they feel?

I borrow the phrase 'exquisite burden' from the writer Arnold Bennet who at the end of the Clayhanger novels describes the hero as 'embracing the exquisite burden of life.' It seems to me that this epithet could be applied to the business of parenting.

Parenting is a burden

There is no getting away from it. From the days when you literally carry your children in your arms or on your back to the days when they are big enough to carry you, to be a parent is to take on a load which at times feels almost unbearably heavy. It is worth pointing out however that most of the bad times are short-lived and are not as serious in the whole scheme of things as they seem at the time. Potty training, the damning school report, the infuriating daily sight of the tip which doubles as a bedroom, the pierced belly button, may cause a tear to be shed and are certainly issues to be faced within the long term training which is your assignment. But the same book of the Bible which says:

> *Train a child in the way he should go, and when he is old he will not turn from it* (Proverbs 22:6),

also says

> *Above all else, guard your heart, for it is the wellspring of life* (Proverbs 4:23).

This is such a helpful reminder of our priority, lest we become bogged down with the external, the mechanical or the frankly superficial and unimportant. It is your child's heart that matters most, especially given the uncertainty of life as pointed out above. You may one day take a sideways glance at your adult offspring and sigh over your evident failure in the area of personal hygiene, table manners or dress sense. But what will be important at the judgment seat of Christ, which our children must face no less than we ourselves? What will best equip your child to face personal crises in his or her life? The answer to those questions will have little to do with being tidy, well-dressed or having A-levels, though those things have undoubted value. So whatever the parenting issue, we need to be always reminded to concentrate on the heart. But finally...

Parenting is exquisite

All four of our children wanted to feature in this book. As a family we happily and frequently discuss the triumphs and disasters of our collective experience. They enjoy the tales of their own waywardness; they enjoy reminding John and myself of times when we got it badly wrong – like the time we got so cross over the ice-creams we bought them at Beachy Head – ice-creams which the gale-force winds swiftly deposited on the ground before a lick was taken! But they also recall with ease and with joy the many games, songs and stories which were a feature of family life. Nobody can take these things away – *Tarzan and the Crocodiles* lives! Last year we were privileged to holiday in Brittany with all our children plus our daughter-in-law and other friends. On our last evening we shared a leisurely meal in a restaurant. I sat back and watched and listened to their lively interaction and I thought – this is what it has been about! You raise people you would be glad to have dinner with! This too is an image of God; this is the agenda for his people:

'Then the angel said to me, 'Write: 'Blessed are those who are invited to the wedding supper of the Lamb!" And he added, 'These are the true words of God.' (Revelation 19:9)

Sharing Jesus with under 5's

How to reach young children with the gospel

Janet Gaukroger

'We're never too young to learn about Jesus! In her book, Sharing Jesus with Under Fives, Janet gives wisdom-packed ways of doing just that. She speaks from the heart of her longing to see under 5's understand the essence of the Christian Faith'

Fiona Castle

"A practical handbook to help you invest in the future"

Rob Parsons

"A very timely and most helpful presentation that fills a need.... long overdue. This has been done by one of the ablest Christian women in Britain."

R.T. Kendall

If you've ever looked at a two-year old and felt totally out of your depth on how to represent the Christian faith to them, this book will help you. Discover the world of the pre-school child, how they think and feel, what each age-group is capable of and then learn how to apply this to teaching them about Christianity. Crèche and Sunday school are not a baby-sitting service but a vital teaching resource for equipping today's church.

Janet Gaukroger has over 20 years experience of teaching children in church under 5.

ISBN 1 85792 672 2

....of Such is the Kingdom

Nurturing Children in the Light of Scripture

Dr. Timothy A. Sisemore

Are you, and your church, bringing up children the way God wants you to?

'Anyone who has a true concern for the spiritual welfare of children in this present age must read this book!'

Mark Johnstone

'Here is a straightforward, readable, challenging and practical manual - just what parents are looking for.'

Sinclair B. Ferguson

'His approach is what the Bible calls wisdom…as rich in Biblical instruction as it is in psychological insight.'

Edmund P. Clowney

Timothy Sisemore builds a practical approach to parenting and children's ministry and shows how to nurture children to be disciples. This is not a theoretical book - if you recognise the need to change your approach he shows you how to do that too.

Timothy A. Sisemore, Ph.D., is Academic Dean and Associate Professor of Counseling at the Psychological Studies Institute in Atlanta and Chattanooga,

ISBN 1 85792 514 9

Christian Focus Publications

publishes books for all ages

Our mission statement –

STAYING FAITHFUL

In dependence upon God we seek to help make his infallible word, the Bible, relevant. Our aim is to ensure that the Lord Jesus Christ is presented as the only hope to obtain forgiveness of sin, live a useful life and look forward to heaven with him.

REACHING OUT

Christ's last command requires us to reach out to our world with his gospel. We seek to help fulfill that by publishing books that point people towards Jesus and for them to develop a Christ-like maturity. We aim to equip all levels of readers for life, work ministry and mission.

Books in our adult range are published in three imprints.

Christian Heritage contains classic writings from the past.
Mentor focuses on books written at a level suitable for Bible College and seminary students, pastors, and other serious readers; the imprint includes commentaries, doctrinal studies, examination of current issues, and church history.
Christian Focus contains popular works including biographies, commentaries, basic doctrine, and Christian living. Our children's books are also published in this imprint.

Christian Focus Publications, Ltd
Geanies House, Fearn, Ross-shire,
IV20 ITW, Scotland, United Kingdom
info@christianfocus.com

For details of our titles visit us on our website
www.christianfocus.com